A WINNING RESUME...

I0486833

The average attention paid in review of a resume is only 7 seconds. Make your 7 seconds count!

The authors herein collectively represent several hundred years' experience with several thousand "employers of choice," hiring hundreds of thousands of candidates nationwide and in more than 100 countries. Recognized as experts by certification authorities and Fortune-rated employers and consistently called upon by the media to include Forbes, the Wall Street Journal, CNN, MSN and more, we know what employers are looking for! Please see our additional credentials and resources at AskHRS.com. Our employer and employee resources have been #1 rated by Google, Yahoo and leading search engines for more than 10 years and top rated in print copy for more than 25 years.

With extensive experience and knowledge on the topic, we have compiled for you answers to the most frequently asked questions and the most common mistakes. The strategies and recommendations within this guide are those that will undoubtedly be most effective in the majority of situations and are the safest in all situations! We at HRS consistently survey and partner with corporate hiring authorities at "employers of choice," and we know what works!

In this newly updated guide we shall discuss the major underlying strategies of winning resume preparation plus precise tactics and examples which best execute those strategies.

Consider the following...

♦ The Internet and software advancements require new practices in resume preparation. We'll teach you how to navigate search engines!

♦ When you do not know who will be screening your resume, you must consider the most common thinking among hiring authorities.

♦ Never make it easier for a resume screener to disqualify your resume than to pass your resume to the next level!

♦ Appeal to the conscious <u>and</u> the subconscious mind. The subconscious can represent 80-90% of brain power!

♦ The goal of the resume is to win you the interview!

Jessica L. Ollenburg, Executive Editor
HRS President and CEO

ISBN: 1-4392-3016-1
Library of Congress Control Number: 2009901865
AskHRS.com

INTRODUCTION

A Winning Resume wins you the next step in the application process. Effectiveness is determined not only by the information presented but also by the manner in which it is presented.

In this guide we will teach you to...
1. Write an effective job objective,
2. Organize your data in a manner which best accentuates your qualifications,
3. Rise to the top in an employer's computer search,
4. Showcase communication skills,
5. Demonstrate desirable behaviors by the method in which you present your resume,
6. Convince the employer that you are worth pursuing, and
7. Win the next step in the selection process.

A resume which does not meet today's standards will disqualify you early from today's hiring process. Employees must sell themselves through persuasion, communication skills, work habits, job focus and attention to detail.

Today's resumes are most often delivered electronically, and many employers now prefer paperless resume intake. Your resume must be "friendly" to whatever IT platform, browser or software application is used by the employer. Simultaneously, your resume must deliver very quickly the information sought by the resume reviewer, or you may find your candidacy overlooked.

To the same extent we recommend a targeted and concise yet powerful resume, this booklet is presented... targeted and concise with powerful information.

TABLE OF CONTENTS

FORMATS, EXAMPLES & SELECTION CRITERIA

Formats presented for your consideration are:

- Targeted
- Functional
- Chronological
- Targeted/Chronological
- Targeted/Functional/Chronological
- Targeted/Functional
- Letter of Application (in lieu of resume)

These formats are highly acceptable and have been developed to effectively accommodate individual work histories. Each format is pertinent to a specific set of circumstances and designed for optimum effectiveness in those circumstances. **Appropriate format selection is critical... the correct format will enable you to maximize your strengths and minimize your weaknesses.**

Targeted

This is an extremely effective resume as it accentuates career "focus" without necessarily distracting from desirable "flexibility" to employer needs. To convince the employer you are certain of career goals is to your advantage. Failure to do so is risky.

This format targets a specific position through use of an objective. All subsequent information strongly supports that objective.

Appropriate to use when one or more apply...

- You know exactly which position or type of job you are pursuing.
- You are considering several different fields of work and are willing to compose a separate resume for each different job you may pursue.
- You know the type of work you want to pursue <u>and</u> your work history may suggest a lack of job stability.
- You want to present related skills and experience gained through volunteer work, school projects or internships.

Do not use when:

- You prefer to use only one resume for a variety of jobs.
- You are not clear about your job direction.

The Job Objective is essential to the effectiveness of the Targeted resume or any combination resume involving the Targeted approach. In today's world of software and personal computer accessibility, an editable electronic version is practical. **The job objective must closely, if not exactly, match the job title to which you are applying.** This may mean an edit every time you send a resume. It is already necessary to edit and customize every cover letter.

Example: Targeted Format

Name
Address
City, State, Zip
Telephone Number
Email

OBJECTIVE: Human Resource Management

SUMMARY:
   Human resource professional offering strong expertise in talent acquisition, organizational development, compensation, benefits, safety, policies, practices and legal compliance.

TARGETED QUALIFICATIONS:
- Ten years progressive Human Resource management, designing, overseeing and/or implementing HR/OD programs for approximately 500 employees, including a support staff of three.
- Manages full cycle talent acquisition programs for all employee classifications.
- Structures and conducts job analyses and created job descriptions congruent with organizational goals and legal compliance.
- Designs, trains in, manages and delivers performance management protocol to effectively drive performance and ensure "no surprises" at review time.
- Cultivates assessment and development programs for leadership, advancement and new hire; selects and coordinates with expert 3rd party assessment centers.
- Responsible for comprehensive benefits administration, including program offerings with annual review and implementation of employee orientation, claims handling and efficiency safeguards.
- Collaborates with executive and departmental teams in strategic design of employer brand, mission and vision; develops communication externally and internally to facilitate competitive advantage and employee relations.
- Researches and conducts compensation reviews in consideration of market conditions; links compensation to job descriptions and performance appraisal instruments.
- Manages payroll function including payroll taxes for entire organization.
- Establishes employee handbook policies compliant with employer culture and legal requirements.
- Creates and administers company-wide safety program.
- Ensures comprehensive legal compliance including record keeping and filings.

WORK HISTORY:
   2000 to Present, Wonderpower, Inc., Phoenix, AZ
   Human Resource Director, 2005 to Present
   Human Resource Manager, 2000 to 2005

   1998 to 2000, Quality Forms, Glendale, AZ
   Human Resource Assistant

EDUCATION:
   B.S. Degree, Human Resource Management
   Arizona State University, 1997

PROFESSIONAL AFFILIATIONS:
   Vice President of Membership, Manager's Roundtable Association, 2007 to Present
   Member, Valley of the Sun Human Resource Association, 1997 to Present

Functional

This resume categorizes skill sets or job functions. This format is very effective when used in combination with the chronological or targeted formats (see examples at the end of this section).

This format may or may not include dates of employment. A functional resume that completely omits employment dates strongly implies poor job stability and should be used with extreme caution! Only omit dates where severe "job hopping" or unexplainable gaps exist to the point of meeting the reader's "worst case expectations."

Appropriate to use when one or more apply...

- You are a recent high school or college graduate with minimum work experience.
- You are re-entering the workforce after a prolonged absence and are open to a variety of positions.
- You may not have much actual paid experience, but want to emphasize skills gained through volunteer work, school projects or internships.
- You wish to emphasize two to four functional areas of skills which you would like to continue using in a new position.
- You are not sure of your career direction or are open to several different areas of work.
- You want to detract from a "job hopping" work history or work gaps.
- You have held positions within the last 10 years which are clearly unrelated to your new career goal.

Do not use when... You have a strong work history, know your job target and could easily relate your background to your job target. Where these conditions exist, please see targeted and/or combination formats.

Example: Functional Format

Name
Address
City, State, Zip
Telephone Number
Email

WORK EXPERIENCE

Assembly/Design/Repair of Robotics
- Performs sub and final assemblies of robots
- Troubleshoots and repairs electrical and mechanical problems
- Designs custom motors from verbal specifications
- Reads and works with blueprints and wiring schematics

Assembly/Design/Repair of Electric Relays
- Assembles and repairs electrical relays for control cabinets
- Winds coils to print specifications using designated fixtures
- Designs fixtures and toolings

General Industrial
- Serves as production operator, set-up technician and line inspector
- Proficient in metric applications and conversions
- Knowledgeable collaborates on shipping, receiving and warehousing teams
- Drives forklift and operates overhead crane

Inventory Control
- Maintains computerized inventory control records for MRP system
- Identifies and resolves inventory control problems
- Problem solves with ordering systems and planning objectives

ACHIEVEMENTS

Awarded for suggesting a method to improve the accuracy of on-hand computer balances which resulted in the identification and recording of $1.8 million of inventory not previously documented.

Suggested a method to automate a seven-function hand operation and improve relay production. Implementation is now in the final stages and is expected to eliminate approximately 24 to 30 jobs.

WORK HISTORY
2008 to Present, The Robotics Company, Milwaukee, WI
Assembler/Robotics and Mechanical

2007 to 2008, Smithson Funeral Home, Milwaukee, WI
Funeral Director

2006 to 2007, The Bradley Company, Milwaukee, WI
Relay Assembler and Warehouse Clerk

EDUCATION
2002 to 2005, University of Wisconsin-Oshkosh
72 credits toward B.S. Degree: Electrical Engineering

Chronological

List work history by dates of jobs performed in reverse chronological order. In other words, most recent employment is listed first.

Appropriate to use when one or more apply:

- You have a strong record of job stability (minimum of two years for each position held).
- There is little redundancy between positions, and each position provides new information related to your candidacy.
- You are open to several different types of positions and want to show your overall experience.
- You have had no more than four jobs over the past 10 years and you will only list those four or less.
- The name of your last employer(s) will add credibility or influence to your credentials.
- You are applying to a high level opportunity and you can reveal a strong progression of advancement through your most recent positions.
- Your job titles are fairly self-explanatory and are directly related to the position you are seeking.

Do not use when:

- Your work history demonstrates a lack of job stability and/or gaps between jobs.
- You are seeking your first job.
- You want to change your field of work and you want to emphasize only certain parts of your work experience.
- You have redundancy in job responsibilities for different jobs you have held and do not want to repeat the listing of these tasks.
- You are re-entering the workforce after a long period of time.

Example: Chronological Format

Name
Address
City, State, Zip
Telephone Number
Email

WORK HISTORY

2005 to Present, A-1 Container Corporation, Tucson, AZ
Customer Service Representative
- Accept customer orders via telephone, data enter and handle inquiries
- Inform customers of prices, shipping dates and other pertinent data
- Follow through on orders to ensure timely delivery
- Respond to problems, investigate and follow through to resolution
- Document account activity and enter data into computer
- Interact with Inventory Department regarding stock orders
- Initiate purchase requisitions

2002 to 2005, Twin Cities Academy, Minneapolis, MN
Gymnastics Coach
- Taught beginner and team gymnastics classes
- Prepared students for state-wide competitions
- Choreographed routine and individual tasks to showcase strength of students
- Tested each student three times annually to determine skill level

2000 to 2002, Westbrook Child Guidance Center, Midwest Homeless Center, and South Hills High
School, Minneapolis, MN
Social Worker/Counselor: Internships
- Constructed programs to enhance social, behavioral, cognitive, interactive and motor skills
- Assisted in design and implementation of mentoring program
- Provided academic tutoring
- Worked with at-risk students, individuals and families in need
- Counseled individuals in goal setting and self esteem

ACHIEVEMENTS

As a gymnastics coach, built classes to exceed anticipated enrollment, increasing enrollment by
approximately 20% annually.

Selected to participate in the regional High School mentoring program, involving a large group of at-
risk and culturally diverse students plus the teachers who volunteered.

Set new record in Village County triathlon completion through focus, determination and training
discipline.

EDUCATION

B.A. Degree in Communications, May 2005
Augsburg College, Minneapolis, MN

Targeted "Combination" Formats

The following combination formats are great for organizing and presenting a high volume of information. Knowing that resumes need to be brief, those of you with strong stability and a high volume of relevant credentials may want to try one of these formats:

Targeted/Chronological
Targeted/Functional/Chronological
Targeted/Functional

Strategies from a combination of formats are used. However, because the targeted format is involved in each, it is essential to know the job to which you are applying.

Before you decide which would be most appropriate for your use, refer to the following guidelines for each combination format to make sure you meet all requirements.

Targeted/Chronological

Overall layout is chronological with targeted format principles. The departure from a traditional chronological format is to use an objective statement with all subsequent information restricted to supporting that objective statement.

Appropriate to use when all following criteria is met:

- You have strong job stability.
- Your work has been concentrated with related skill sets, industry or career field.
- You know the type of work or the job for which you are applying.

Do not use when:

- You are seeking your first job.
- You have a "job hopping" work history and/or gaps in your employment.
- You want to make a career change.

Example: Targeted/Chronological Format

Name
Address
City, State, Zip
Telephone Number
Email

OBJECTIVE: Business Development Management

EXPERIENCE:

2001 to Present
National Food Distributors, Inc., Los Angeles, CA
Sales and Marketing Director
- Designs and communicates marketing plans for new territories
- Directs comprehensive operations of Sales and Marketing functions
- Manages sales force of ten plus service and purchasing staff of five
- Approves all procurement, merchandising, pricing, marketing, research and timing decisions

1994 to 2001
Institutional Foods, Inc., Los Angeles, CA
District Sales Manager
- Hired, trained and supervised sales force of five
- Established and accomplished objectives and goals for start-up market
- Introduced concepts and trained staff in consultative selling, value-added programs and customer service

ACHIEVEMENTS:

- Achieved #1 status in the organization for return on investment for four consecutive years
- Pioneered major marketing projects with results exceeding established goals by 34%
- Designed and implemented programs which moved the company from existing declining markets to new growth oriented markets with results in increased gross margins to 20% above industry average
- Reduced overall sales and marketing expenses by 25% while exceeding set sales goals
- Introduced innovative sales concepts which focus on quotas, motivation and customer service with indications to date showing results in excess of set goals

EDUCATION:

Bachelor of Business Administration Degree in Marketing
University of California at Berkeley, 1989

Business Development Courses including:
Public Speaking, Negotiation, Creative Selling Skills, Creative Sales Management, Territory
    Management and Marketing Research, 1994 to Present

Targeted/Functional/Chronological

The Chronological influence is reflected in the overall physical layout or format. Targeted refers to the objective statement and that all subsequent resume content relates to and supports that objective. The functional portion of this format is the grouping and labeling of job tasks into specific functions.

Appropriate to use when:

♦ You have had only one previous employer and it has been of two or more years' duration with a variety of responsibilities that are all pertinent to the job for which you are applying.

♦ You have a strong record of job stability and you want to stay in that same field/industry. Your work has been concentrated in the same field with variety and progression of responsibilities.

♦ You qualify for either of the above two reasons but also want to emphasize the names of employer(s) for whom you have worked. This would be especially important if your previous employer(s) can be easily recognized.

Do not use when:

♦ You are seeking your first job.
♦ You have a "job hopping" work history or gaps in your employment.
♦ You are re-entering the workforce after a long period of time.
♦ You want to make a career change and want to minimize your current industry background or emphasize only certain aspects of your previous job(s).

Example: Targeted/Functional/Chronological Format

Name
Address
City, State, Zip
Telephone Number
Email

OBJECTIVE: Materials Management, Health Care Industry

SUMMARY OF QUALIFICATIONS: Highly dedicated professional with eleven year record of consistent achievement in the design, direction and implementation of Purchasing, Receiving, Warehousing and Printing operations of a major metropolitan hospital.

WORK HISTORY:
   1998 to Present, Memorial Hospital, New York, NY
   Director of Purchasing, 2003 to Present
   Administrative Coordinator, 1998 to 2003

   ADMINISTRATION
   - Directs overall operations of Purchasing, Receiving, Warehousing and in-house printing functions
   - Serves on the Hospital Executive Committee with jurisdiction for all purchasing and related functions

   PURCHASING/DISTRIBUTION
   - Manages annual purchasing budget of $6,000,000
   - Negotiates and/or approves all contracts for commodities and capital equipment
   - Oversees distribution of inventory and equipment purchases

   GRAPHICS PRODUCTION
   - Schedules, reviews and sets priorities for all internal graphics projects, both print and electronic/web-based
   - Coordinates production team and collaborates in performance management activities
   - Examines work to ensure conformity to individual departmental specifications

ACHIEVEMENTS:
   - Established competitive bidding procedures which resulted in a 32% savings in purchases over the previous contract period.
   - Established an in-house printing and photography department which improved turn-around time on requests by 74% and realized average annual savings of $220,000 over a five-year period.
   - Implemented a computerized inventory system for access to daily stock levels which allowed for more efficient inventory planning and control, as well as, improved cash flow.

EDUCATION:
   M.B.A., Loyola University, Chicago, Illinois, 1997
   B.S.B.A., New York University, New York, New York, 1994

PROFESSIONAL AFFILIATIONS:
   American Production and Inventory Control Society (APICS)
   New York Purchasing Management Association (NYPMA)

Targeted/Functional

Probably our favorite! This format targets a specific job through use of an objective statement <u>and</u> specific categories of skill sets which support that objective.

Appropriate to use when:

♦ Conditions are met for the targeted format, **and...**
♦ You know exactly which position or type of job you are seeking and this position requires knowledge and experience in not just one, but a variety of functions.

Do not use when:

♦ You prefer to use only one resume for a variety of jobs.
♦ You are not clear about your job direction.

Example: Targeted/Functional Format

Name
Address
City, State, Zip
Telephone Number
Email

OBJECTIVE: Business Development, Health Care Industry

QUALIFICATIONS:

Business Development and Communications
- 5 years direct sales of medical consumables
- Builds relationships with physicians, medical facility teams and patients
- Prepares and presents sales proposals and reports
- Creates instructional materials
- Develops and conducts presentations to individuals and large groups
- Expands client base through dedication to and recognition of client needs

Health Care
- 14 years health care experience
- Health care environment experience to include hospitals, nursing homes, private homes and public health
- Knowledgeable with care for patients of all ages and in a variety of health care environments

ACHIEVEMENTS:

- Increased territory sales 37% through development of new and inactive accounts
- Ranked second within entire organization for annual sales production for 2007 and 2008

WORK HISTORY:

2004 to Present, Midtown Medical Group, Las Vegas, NV
Account Executive

2000 to 2004, Westcity Hospital, Las Vegas, NV
Licensed Practical Nurse

1998 to 2000, Western Lakes Department of Health, Las Vegas, NV
Public Health Technician

1995 to 1998, Rolling Hills West Nursing Home, Las Vegas, NV
Licensed Practical Nurse

EDUCATION/LICENSING:

Licensed Practical Nurse, 1995
Las Vegas Nursing College, Las Vegas, NV

Letter of Application

This is a combination resume and cover letter. It is recommended for younger persons with little or no work history.

The value of the resume letter is that it calls attention away from lack of credentials/experience and presents the positive attributes of the candidate. The strategy is to demonstrate strong knowledge of and interest in the company and present a straightforward appeal by declaring very precisely just what you can do for the company. This can be very effective for those who can prove a strong work ethic without much work history.

Appropriate to use when:

♦ You have in-depth knowledge of the company and the job for which you are applying.
♦ You want to work at that particular company and could communicate your reason(s).
♦ You know the person or persons in charge of hiring. (It could be the Human Resource Director or it may be a specific department manager.)
♦ You have training, coursework or skills that would be beneficial to the company.
♦ A resume would disqualify you because your work history does not meet the job requirements.

Do not use when... You do not meet all of the above criteria.

Example: Letter of Application

January 12, 2009

Mr. Robert Browne, V.P. Press Operations
Print/Graphics, Inc.
2200 West Capitol Drive
Peoria, IL 60340

Dear Mr. Browne:

I was given your name by the Meghan Brown and I am writing to ask for your assistance. I want very much to work in the printing industry and especially in your organization. I understand that Print/Graphics, Inc. is the fastest growing and most progressive printing firm in this area. Specifically, I am interested in a training program that would offer me the opportunity to eventually become a press operator.

I am presently interning with Milestone Graphics as a trainee in a comprehensive production program. Some of my responsibilities include:

* paper cutter   * stapling   * camera
* stripping   * fold   * paper jogger
* press operation (multilith 1250)   * errands/phone

My education also supports my career goal as I have just finished the first year of a two-year Associate degree program in Printing and Graphic Arts at Peoria Area Technical College. Courses completed are:

* Printing and Publishing   * Photography
* ½ Toner Techniques   * Printer's Math
* Graphic Communication Process (stripping)   * General Liberal Arts

With intention to complete this program within 18 months, I will schedule my coursework around my employment. Classes are available evenings and weekends.

I believe it is important you know that I am a hard working, sincere and very responsible person. I have steadily worked and attended school simultaneously since age 16. While in high school and during summer breaks, I have performed such work as cooking, painting houses, remodeling houses, janitorial, and I have consistently demonstrated a strong work ethic.

A chance to personally meet with you and interview for a position would be greatly appreciated. I will call next week to hopefully schedule an appointment.

Thank you for your time and consideration.

Sincerely,

(signature)

Name
Telephone
Email

CATEGORIES OF INFORMATION

Past Employers and Dates of Employment

List dates of employment, the name, city and state of employers and your job title for each position held. Use reverse chronological order... listing most recent first.

Part-time or Temporary positions... Most employers will not consider it omission or falsification to exclude these employment listings from your resume. However, if they explain a noticeable gap in your employment or add to your credentials, you may choose to include them. The "Highlights," "Qualifications" or skill sets sections or Targeted, Functional or combination formats allow you to list the career related skills/accomplishments gained from those positions without need to list the employment details. As the resume is not a legal document such as an official employment application, you have more discretion here in what you choose to disclose.

One of the first things an employer looks for is likely job stability. Starting and ending dates of past positions are of critical interest to the prospective employer. In situations where you have held a position for a very short period of time, you may want to omit that entire job information from your resume. However, if you list the position, you must also list the dates of that position. When deciding to omit a short term position, consider the gap which may be created. Also consider that if your resume is successful, you will be asked to complete an application, which is a legal document requiring your signature. Only temporary or part-time jobs are customarily allowable as excluded from your application.

If each job spans multiple years, then months do not need not to be listed. If your job stability qualifies you to do so, omitting months will give the reader a quick sense of your stable work history.   If each job in your listed employment history does not span multiple years, then you should include the months as long as you are not revealing frequent and inexplicable gaps in employment. If your work stability is strong, you may wish your years of employment to be listed first. If not so strong, you may wish to list them after the company name or job title. Parallelism and consistency are important. Use the same order throughout the section.

A resume is expected to reflect up to 10 years of work experience. Those of you with less than 10 years experience should present your entire work history, especially full time permanent positions. Those with more than 10 years experience need only present information related to your past 10 employment years. Exception rules follow:

- If you worked 10 or more years in your present position, include 1 or 2 positions which immediately preceded your present employment, spanning up to 20 years of work history, preferably related to your present career.
- If you held a related position more than 10 years ago and you have had no more than 4 positions since, you may include that position. By doing so, you must also list all full time permanent positions since.
- If you have had a large mix of positions, some career related and some not, you may re-title your employment history category "Career Related" or "Targeted" Employment History and include only relevant employment.   Beware of creating questionable employment gaps and/or implying poor job stability. It may be advisable to also list another section of "Other" Employment to close the gaps.
- If you are returning to the work force after hiatus and you offer a prior history of career related work experience, you may include your prior employment history considering each rule presented here.

- If you are at an executive level, you may wish to show a pattern of growth which would benefit from additional work history listed.

The Objective Statement

With the amount of training and investment asked of an employer, **it is essential to convince the employer that the position you are applying for precisely matches your career goals.** Turnover hurts most employers! An objective statement is essential with the targeted or combination targeted resume, and it is strongly preferred with chronological, functional and letters of application. In very specific and concise language, it conveys career focus and properly routes the resume to the appropriate hiring authority. The statement "sets the agenda" for the entire resume. It is the concise "thesis statement." Therefore, all subsequent information must pertain to and support that objective. Examples follow:

OBJECTIVE: Human Resources
OBJECTIVE: Human Resource Manager
OBJECTIVE: Human Resources Management, Health Care

In these examples, the title "Human Resource Manager" signifies strength and experience in the area of human resources and can be used for any industry or organization. By stating "Manager," this candidate might not be considered for any HR support role positions. When specifying the desired industry, as in the third example, the writer should have strong human resource experience in a health care environment. By stating "Health Care," this candidate might not be considered for any HR positions outside of the health care field.

OBJECTIVE: CNC Operator
OBJECTIVE: Pharmaceutical Sales Representative
OBJECTIVE: Business Development

Again, the above objectives are very clear and concise. They tell the reader at a glance exactly the type of position the writer is pursuing. This is imperative. Be sure to read the job advertisement closely to best determine what the employer is looking for and customize the objective for each individual organization. You want to capture the reader's interest and encourage that person to read your entire resume.

Incorrect Use... Too often we see long, rambling objectives that do not refer to a specific position. This is a very dangerous way to start a resume. The writer is surely setting the reader up for a negative reaction. Generally, the reader will have numerous resumes to read and will, most likely, become frustrated just trying to identify the job for which the writer is applying, especially if the reader has a number of position openings. An example of the type of inappropriate objective to which we are referring:

"A position in a stable, growing company that offers challenge, responsibility and the opportunity for growth and allows me to utilize my skills and education."

What job or type of job is the writer seeking? Is the applicant questioning the prospective employer's stability and growth? Employers typically find such a statement to be annoying and unfocused. At a minimum, such a statement is meaningless and, therefore, it is likely that these resumes will not get serious attention.

Another example of incorrect use is when the resume presents miscellaneous job history information and then uses an objective statement in an attempt to target a specific job. This can be very damaging to the applicant. When a job preference is indicated, the reader will expect to find specific job-related experience and qualifications. If this information is not present, the assumption will be that the desired qualifications do not exist and, most likely, will result in the disqualification of the resume (and you) from further consideration.

Do not use an objective statement unless it relates to and is validated by evidence presented in your resume... and do not assume that you have no evidence to offer. Even if you're just starting out or seeking a total career change, you probably have more to offer than you realize. Many skills are transferable and sometimes... personal characteristics, aptitudes or work ethic are more important to an employer than your specific work history and training.

Side note: Avoid the word "utilize" altogether in your objective. As described herein, it has no place, and quite frankly, it's an overused cliché which at times can create either amusement or annoyance due to the meaningless overuse.

Summary or Highlights of Qualifications

The "Summary" or "Highlights of Qualifications" is used as an introduction to your resume. It is placed immediately after the name and address or immediately after the objective statement, depending upon the format you are using. The strategy is to quickly announce strengths you bring to the job, grabbing the reader's interest and setting expectations so he/she will want to read on.

Although the qualifications information is presented at the beginning of the resume, it may be most easily written **after** you have completed a rough draft of your resume. Once the draft is assembled, you will have a condensed and concentrated version of your work experience along with other critical credentials. A quick analysis of this orderly information will allow you to easily recognize your most significant qualifications which you can then summarize or highlight for immediate reader impact.

Work experience, as well as, space availability should be considered when you decide whether to present your qualifications through a summary or through use of a bullet-pointed highlights section.

Summary of Qualifications... The summary of qualifications is a synthesis of one's overall work experience and accomplishments. It should be used by those with extensive experience and skills. It is appropriate to use with any format and should be written in paragraph style. Statements should be brief and refer to years of experience, skills and accomplishments. Educational credentials, if pertinent to the position you are seeking, may also be quickly presented. Again, this is a summary so information should be brief and presented in approximately one to four brief sentences. This style presentation is ideal for lengthy resumes as it requires very little space.

Highlights of Qualifications... This section differs from the summary in several ways. Rather than paragraph style, the format consists of quick bulleted statements. It can be used by both those with strong, as well as, those with limited experience. As opposed to being primarily a synthesis of the overall work experience, emphasis can also be on individual strengths. This may include information related to experience, achievements, skills, education and/or personal characteristics. Qualifications may be drawn from listed employment history, unlisted employment history, volunteer or community based work, personal hobby, education or personal research... and you must be willing to support the statement if granted an interview. Those with extensive experience can use this section to quickly and concisely convey strengths and accomplishments which might otherwise have been lost or overlooked in paragraph format. Those with limited job related employment experience can use this section to set forth credentials gained through other personal experience. Also, because with limited experience it can sometimes be difficult to generate information sufficient to fill one entire page, this method of presentation requires approximately 2+ inches of space and serves to very effectively stretch a resume.

When Using with a Targeted Format... Guidelines are basically the same. The exception is that all references to work history and education must support your job objective. This is a great opportunity to immediately present your credentials and reinforce your job objective.

Examples:

For any format except targeted:
Summary of Qualifications
12 years experience in manufacturing environment. In-depth knowledge of materials requirement planning (MRP), inventory control, customer service and inside sales functions. Twice recognized as "Employee of the Month" for outstanding work contributions.

For targeted format:
(Objective: Office Management/Bookkeeping)
Summary of Qualifications
Innovative administrator with 20 years of office management experience. Strong accounting support and computer skills. Proven record of highly effective and creative problem solving, organizational and leadership abilities. Reputation for promoting and maintaining a positive, productive and results-driven work environment.

For any format:
Highlights of Qualifications
* 4 years of continuous part-time and seasonal employment while in school.
* Strong work ethic with proven record of commitment and dedication to employer and job tasks.
* Ability to develop and maintain rapport with wide variety of people.
* Works well independently or as team member.
* Strong communication skills including written, verbal and listening.

For targeted format:
(Objective: Entry Level Public Relations position)
Highlights of Qualifications
* Experienced in writing press releases and working with various media.
* Excellent writing, speaking and active listening skills.
* Creative and enthusiastic with ability to impact positively on others.
* Strong commitment to quality and customer satisfaction.
* Spanish language fluency in both oral and written communications.
* B.A. degree with double major in Communications and Marketing.

Both qualifications and achievements can be listed on your resume. However, if space is limited, the Achievements section should take priority. Achievements are discussed in detail later.

Job Tasks

Job tasks, often line items within a job description, are the actual tasks or duties you perform to accomplish the objectives and goals of your job. These refer to two separate areas of knowledge and skills:

Functional: Knowledge and skills gained through performance of usual and customary job functions.

Technical: Knowledge and skills gained through specific training and apply to the operation of equipment and/or the performance of highly specialized job functions.

It is the presentation of job tasks on your resume that will provide the reader with the most information regarding your experience, knowledge and skills. Because this is extremely vital information, great attention and effort should be given to the documentation of these tasks. Write each task in statement form. Condense your statements to one line, if possible, to conserve space.

If you do not know your job target... Document tasks from present, as well as, all previous positions. Start with your most recent position. Think about what you do each day from the time you start your job until you have finished. List all job tasks. Repeat this exercise for each position you have held.

Once documentation of your entire work history is complete, review the statements to determine which you will use on your resume. If you find statements which refer to similar tasks, combine without redundancy and be sure to include the one that describes greater responsibility. Also, be careful to use those statements that most accurately reflect your current abilities and eliminate those that represent elementary skills and/or abilities you may have surpassed.

If you have identified your job target... If you know the position or type of position you intend to seek, then requirements for documentation of your work history differ slightly. You will still list the dates, names and locations of all employers and your job titles. However, it will be necessary to list only those tasks that relate to and support the job sought. In this case you will be using a targeted or combination targeted format, and this requires only information which relates to and supports your job objective.

Documentation of Numbers... It is very important to first consider if numbers can be used to your advantage. Strong numbers that do not overpower you for the position should be used whenever possible. Where you decide to use numbers, consider documenting the number of people you supervise or affect. Consider detailing budget or savings amounts. Use the number which targets and presents you most favorably. Numbers are considered "hard facts" and strengthen a resume. Eliminate numbers if you believe they are not impressive. Be careful not to exaggerate or oversell yourself. If the number is important to the employer, you will most likely need to substantiate it at some point.

Documentation of Technical Skills... Most jobs require some technical skill. For instance, office positions often require skill in operation of routine equipment such as calculators, copy, fax and/or mail machines. Assumptions regarding skill in operation of these will be made by the reader. Mention of these skills may actually minimize your credentials.

More advanced technical skills related to computer operations, software and other high tech, engineering or manufacturing equipment will be of interest and should be presented.

Because the use of computers is universal, we recommend that you present any computer related skills you might possess, no matter what type of position you are seeking. The amount of space/time you devote to your computer proficiency should be directly correlated to the amount of time you would likely spend using computer in the job to which you are applying. Documentation of skills should be very brief and to-the-point as in the following examples:

- Software proficiency in PeopleSoft, Quickbooks, Adobe Creative Suite, Microsoft Word, Excel, PowerPoint and Publisher.
- Set up and operate lathes, mills, surface grinders, drill presses and boring bars.
- Program, set up and operate Okuma-Howi and Mazak CNC mills and lathes.

Placement of Technical Skills on Your Resume... This information can be integrated with your functional task statements or placed in a separate category titled "Technical Skills." Information can be presented in one of two ways:

- Integrate technical skills with task statements when you have only one or two lines of information to present.
- Present technical skills as a separate category: 1) when you have three or more lines of information to present, or 2) when your job responsibilities are comprised primarily of technical skills.

Achievements

Definition: Job-Related Achievements... Achievements are contributions you have made, awards/recognition earned and/or leadership roles you have held. An achievement could be something you have done on the job that you consider to be "above and beyond" your everyday job responsibilities. Think about special projects which you have been selected to perform, are proud of, and/or believe have had beneficial results for your employer(s).

Definition: Other Types of Achievements... Other types of achievements could be related to your academic history, elected positions in professional organizations and/or community groups, or any other contributions you may have made or recognition received in the community or "world at large."

Importance of Achievements... Achievement statements demonstrate your ability to produce results and provide proof of highly desirable personal qualities such as leadership, initiative, creativity, dedication, work ethic, problem solving, and productivity. It is this information that is likely to gain the prospective employer's interest.

Strategies for Generating Achievement Statements... Those of you most likely to have "achieved" on the job will be those in the continuing worker category. It is reasonable to expect that the longer you have been in the workforce, the greater your chances will be for achievement.

For those with little or no experience, it will, most likely, be difficult to generate work-related achievement statements. But if you have any experience at all, do not give up. Do not just expect not to have achieved. You must try to identify your contributions. Read the following strategies and give it your best effort. Employers will be pleased to read of any on-the-job achievements and certainly will not expect them to be of the same magnitude as those presented by more experienced workers.

Strategies: Experienced/Continuing Workers... Consider any contributions you may have made in the following areas:

- Company savings due to your actions/ideas regarding cost, time, space, human capital or materials.
- Increased profits.
- Sales quotas exceeded or consistently met.
- New business generated.
- Quality improvement regarding product, service, or workplace.
- Quantifiable improvement to employee retention, motivation and engagement.
- Awards or recognition earned.
- Promotions received within a short time span or multiple promotions received showing progression of career.
- Incidents where you were chosen to introduce, implement or lead others in any new procedures, policies or systems.
- Inventions or patents attained as a direct result of your individual or team effort.
- Any action or idea suggested by you that was adopted and implemented by the company.
- Any new program or procedure that you created, developed and/or implemented with improved bottom-line results.

Strategies: Workers with Little or No Experience... When trying to identify on-the-job achievements, we suggest you consider the following:

- Any on-the-job performance which created positive impact beyond expectations for your employer.
- Anything you may have done at work for which you were given special recognition or praise.
- Any suggestion you may have made which resulted in the improvement of a task or procedure that was accepted and implemented by your employer.
- Have you solved an existing or diffused a potential problem regarding a client, co-worker, or company policy or procedure?
- Have you saved the company time and/or money with improved procedures?
- Have you created/implemented any new systems, e.g. filing, inventory, computer, bookkeeping, shipping, receiving, warehousing, etc?
- Have you done anything to improve the quality of service, product, procedures or work environment?
- Did you perform the same job as others and do it in less time or with less expense?
- Have you won any awards for exceeding quotas, e.g. sales, attendance, quality, or quantity of work performed?
- Did you identify a specific need and/or suggest remedies?
- Were you part of a team or group that produced above-average results for a project or report?
- Have you ever received an exceptional job evaluation?

Recording of Achievement Statements... Documentation should be results-oriented and, if possible, contain quantitative information.

- Write achievement statements in short paragraph style. One or two brief sentences is ideal.
- Prioritize achievements and list in order of importance.
- Use numbers whenever possible.
- List work-related achievements first. Follow with achievements related to internships, volunteer work, etc.
- Educational achievements should be used only by recent graduates and placed in the Education section of the resume.

Document your title, action taken and the positive results. Be careful to document information accurately. If you cannot remember exact numbers, then use an approximate number and say it is an approximate number. Use dates if they are recent and you can use them consistently in a positive manner throughout the section.

Education

Typically listed in reverse chronological order (most recent first), you may decide to downplay or omit coursework that fails to enhance your strengths or makes you appear unfocused as to career objective.

Degree/Diploma Recipients... The attainment of a degree, even if not job related, speaks highly to your accomplishment, skill set and commitment to learning. It is entirely up to you how you present this. If your major or minor is completely unrelated, it is most likely to your advantage to omit this information. Contrarily, you may elect more detail if related. Year of completion is customary and typically only omitted where you believe your age is not a strength. Be careful, however, because the skilled resume reader knows that omission of date implies negative information. If you are involved in, have completed some coursework or have received your Master's, J.D., Ph.D., or other advanced degree, then this information should be listed before undergraduate coursework or bachelor's degree.

Degree/Diploma Candidates... If you are currently enrolled in or have taken some college courses but have not yet graduated, provide detail to the extent your coursework is attractive to the employer. Unless applying for internship or contract position with defined end date before you graduate, be careful your detailed major does not imply you will resign employment upon program completion. You may wish to omit major or part-time schooling that is obviously unrelated. Where you choose to detail this coursework, the following guidelines should be considered:
- If you have completed three plus years of full-time schooling and are not currently a student, state the dates of attendance and/or the number of credits you have earned.
- If you have completed three years or more of part-time schooling and are not currently a student, state the dates of attendance.
- If you have completed less than three years and are not currently a student, simply list the dates of attendance.
- If you are currently a student with candidacy to graduate within the next two years, and the position relates to your degree, state your anticipated date of graduation.
- If you have a bachelor's degree, state your degree even though you may have also completed a portion of or an entire postgraduate program. Major area(s) of study need only be listed if job-related.

High School Graduates... Use only if you have not had any college coursework. List only the fact that you are a high school graduate, along with the name, city and state of the school. Dates of graduation reveal your age, so do not provide this information if you do not want to reveal your age. Do not reveal your age unless you are certain the employer has an ideal age in mind, and you fit that profile. High school coursework should only be mentioned if extraordinary job-related training was gained through high school less than 10 years ago.

Job-Specific Workshops/Seminars... Most employees, at some time in their careers, have had the benefit of attending various job-related workshops and/or seminars. Even though these programs may be beneficial to the job which you are seeking, we recommend the following:

- If you have strong credentials: this information is optional.
- If you are struggling to fill space on a resume: use this information. However, only if you have very limited credentials should you list each seminar/workshop separately. It is better to simply state, after the listing of other educational credentials, that you have attended various workshops and seminars and their general topics. With a targeted resume, you will only add this information if it supports your job objective.

> Example: Loyola Marymount University, Continuing Education
> Attended numerous labor law workshops and seminars, 2000 - 2006

Educational programs sponsored by universities and colleges and highly respected professional organizations e.g. the Institute of Management Consultants (IMC) and the American Production and Inventory Control Society (APICS) are generally assumed to be of "high quality" and, therefore, favorably regarded. If the seminars or workshops you attended were sponsored by these types of institutions, then by all means, present this information. It is not necessary, however, to list other sponsors such as private companies or groups. In these situations you may simply state:

> 2000 - 2006, Labor Law Workshops and Continuing Education Seminars

Other Seminars/Workshops... You will have to do some differentiating here. Topics of programs related to personal interests, such as crafts or astrology may enhance your personal life, but unless they can directly contribute to the job for which you are applying, do not present them. On the other hand, personal enrichment courses such as public speaking, written communications, leadership or other personal skills enhancements would certainly have universal appeal. These programs will strengthen your resume and add value for the employer. By all means, list them. Again, however, only a general reference should be made.

> Example: 2004 - 2005, University of Southern California
> Workshops: Business Writing and Active Listening Skills

Adult Education/Non-Degreed Coursework... Follow guidelines given for Workshops and Seminars.

Military History

Any Format Except Targeted... Treat work performed in the military the same as any other work. List the dates and name of service, your rank, job title and job tasks. Extraordinary rank progression should be presented as an achievement.
When assembling your resume, presentation of this information will depend upon the format you select and should be included with all other job information. However, if you prefer, you may simply list this information under the heading of Military History and provide information regarding the dates and name of service. Mention of your rank is optional.

Targeted Format... If you are writing a targeted resume and the work you performed in the service is related to your current job objective, then include the task information with your other work experiences.   The dates, names of service, your rank and job title would be listed separately in the Work History section. However, if this experience is not job-related, then you can use a separate category entitled Military History and limit the information to dates and name of service. Mention of your rank would be optional.

Licenses/Certifications

List those job-related licenses and certifications that add strength and credibility to your credentials. To convince the employer of your stable interest in the position you are applying for, be careful which licenses you present. Examples follow:

Real Estate License
Use when: You are applying for any real estate or property-related position.
Do not use when: Real estate sales is your second job. A prospective employer might believe this would be a distraction from your primary job. Also, if not job-related, a prospective employer might infer that because you have taken time to get this license, you are unsure of your professional goals.

Cosmetology License
Use when: You are applying for any position related to cosmetology.
Do not use when: You are seeking any position other than that related to cosmetology. The employer will worry about your focus and intentions for job longevity.

Pilot License
Use on any resume. This licensing process is quite difficult and suggests initiative, perseverance and intelligence. Also, this additional credential will not necessarily detract from your career or job performance.

Bartender License
Do not use on any resume except for a related position. You could very well be "tapping into" someone's bias regarding alcohol and preconceived ideas regarding behavior.

Certified Nursing Assistant
Use when: You are applying for any health care related position.
Do not use when: You are applying for a job not related to the medical field. Employers will think that you are just looking for a job to "fill in" until you can find something in the medical field.

Professional/Community Involvement

Like achievement statements, memberships and offices held in professional and/or community organizations tell a convincing story of desired personality traits, such as leadership, work ethic, dedication, teamwork, interaction skills and sense of responsibility. Use this information readily as it will certainly promote a positive image for you.

Personal Information

Details related to height, weight, age, family status, hobbies, interests or other personal items should not be included on your resume. It's simply unwise to give an employer info not lawful to have toward your candidacy. Not only are these known discriminatory factors, protected by Equal Employment Opportunity laws, but providing this information backfires against the candidate more often than not. If you know for certain this information will positively affect your candidacy, insert it into the cover letter. Also, remember that the goal of the resume is to get the interview. Personal information can project the illusion that the reader now has enough information about you to make a hiring decision without interviewing you. Such an illusion can only disqualify you.

References

Most employers believe references should never be referred to on a resume. Most often we see the statement: "References furnished upon request." The mention of references at this point is cliché, meaningless and premature. If interested, an employer will assume that if asked, you will furnish references. It is helpful however to have a typed list of references readily available at the time of interview just in case this information is requested. Please avoid providing references without first being asked. Appearing overanxious to provide specific names implies to many employers that you have "set up" or "hand-picked" your references, destroying the credibility of those references.

COMMUNICATING YOUR MESSAGE

The Reader's Perception

As true in any written communication, the best strategy is to write with the reader in mind. This means that you must consider not only what you say and how you say it, but how it will impact the reader. All work involved in producing a resume would be fruitless if, in the end, the reader would be unable to accurately interpret the message as you intended.

You must analyze everything you write and try to see it as the reader will. Most likely, the reader will be someone who knows nothing about you and will learn only from what you write. It will be up to you to ensure that he or she will understand your intended meaning and be favorably impressed as well.

The most qualified people to provide you second opinion are those who have been successful as a hiring authority, especially in a position similar to that which you are applying. Be careful here, because being successful for one or two similar employers still doesn't guarantee that individual understands or agrees with the hiring authority you need to impress. Employers own different cultures, perceptions and ideas of what works best. This, in fact, is why we wrote this book... to offer you experience in what works with thousands of employers, not just one, two or three. Professional writers without this perspective may be unable to truly understand the reader's perception.

The Power of Language

Because of tremendous space limitations on your resume, each word written is critical. Your entire resume is best presented on **1 to 1½ pages.** (Only rare exceptions allow the ability to exceed 2 pages without potentially immediately disqualifying yourself with some resume screeners.) In that limited framework, your goal is to portray yourself as competently and favorably as possible.

With careful attention to the following strategies you should be able to accomplish that goal:

- Be concrete, crisp and vigorous in your word choice. Use words that convey an accurate and clear message.
- Say what you have to say as briefly and clearly as possible. Condense information to major points and allow for some assumptions by the reader.
- Always take the opportunity to complete each statement with meaningful and descriptive words. And lastly, do not use the first person style, never use words such as "I", and "me" or "my" except in your cover letter or letter of application.
- Use concise and precise statements. When listing your experience or capabilities, always begin each sentence with the strongest and most accurate action verb possible. Start each sentence with a different action verb. Redundancy is boring and certainly less than creative.

Expectations for clarity and presentation are very demanding. Today, more than ever, there is an awareness of the importance of strong communication skills. While your resume is being reviewed for job-related skills and abilities, the reader will also be evaluating your ability to express yourself in a clear, concise and informative manner.

Action Verbs and Examples

In addition to words used throughout examples herein, the following is a list of action verbs to which you can refer. Choose clear, meaningful and results-oriented words wherever you can.

achieved	correlates	interviews	reduce
accounts	counseled	invented	referred
accomplish	decreased	involved	renovate
accumulate	define	issued	repairs
acquire	delegate	joined	represents
activate	delivered	justified	reshape
administer	designs	lectures	research
advanced	detected	led	resolves
advised	determined	lessened	restore
allocated	develops	logged	restructure
analyzes	devised	maintained	reverse
appraise	diagnoses	manage	reviews
approve	directed	market	revitalize
arrange	displayed	master	routed
arbitrated	distributed	maximize	saved
assign	documented	mentored	schedules
assemble	edited	met	screened
assumed	eliminated	minimized	secured
attend	engineers	modify	selected
audits	enhances	monitor	serves
authorize	ensured	motivate	solved
automate	established	navigate	standardize
authored	evaluated	negotiates	stimulate
budgeted	examines	obtained	streamlines
built	expanded	operates	strengthen
calculated	expedite	orchestrate	structured
catalog	focus	ordered	studied
change	forecast	organized	submitted
charted	formulate	oversee	supervised
coaches	founded	participate	supplied
communicates	function	perform	systemize
compile	generate	persuade	teaches
completed	guarantee	pioneered	test
composed	heads	plan	trace
computes	identified	prepare	tracks
conceptualize	implemented	presents	trained
conducted	improved	process	translate
conserved	increased	produce	trim
consolidated	initiates	proposed	update
constructed	innovate	provides	upgrade
consults	installed	promoted	undertook
contracted	institutes	publish	validates
contributed	instructs	qualify	verifies
controls	integrate	realize	vitalized
coordinates	interpreted	record	wrote

Understanding Search Engines

Technical terminology and industry "keywords" are essential! Ensure that keywords found in the recruitment posting are present in your resume. Look also to recruitments and job descriptions for similar positions and ensure those keywords are additionally present. Be certain to include in your resume the key terms which might be used in a database search. However, be careful to avoid the use of acronyms unless used after the full spelling of the name. It is best to include both acronym and full spelling to ensure your resume comes up no matter what the search criteria. Abbreviations and parentheses should also be avoided.

Construct a Rough Draft

Construct a rough draft of your resume so you can critique your work before you write the final product. Review your draft with an eye to the following:

Word Choice: Descriptive Statements
Examine words you have used to describe yourself and ask yourself the following questions:
♦   Do my words convey a pertinent and interesting message?
♦   Do my words accurately and actively represent my skills and achievements?
♦   Am I satisfied with the image I present of myself?

If you are not sure, think about what it is you would like the reader to know about you. Think about what you, as an individual, can bring to the job; how you can personally contribute. Think about how you would like to be perceived by the reader. Use words that convey your intended message. For instance, active verbs you might use if you think of yourself as a:
♦   Leader: directed, organized, planned, controlled
♦   Team Player: collaborated, conferred, participated, assisted, contributed, served
♦   Creative: designed, created, conceptualized
♦   Change Champion: negotiated, persuaded, advocated

Word Choice: Overall Message
♦   Appropriate and parallel verb tense... present or past
♦   Concise and precise message
♦   Clarity of intended message
♦   Parallel construction of sentences

Punctuation... Proper punctuation is essential. Not only does it demonstrate sound English and writing skills, attention to detail, and an accuracy ethic; but it also provides for easy and uninterrupted reading. Review your punctuation. If you are not sure of the accuracy, enlist the aid of someone who can help. Most software programs will provide assistance.

Spell Check... PLEASE use this feature as it demonstrates attention to detail, at a minimum. With the abundance of spelling tools available in today's software programs, the only excuse for misspellings is, in fact, lack of attention to detail. Because some misspellings create actual words, please read through to ensure accuracy.

Resume Length

The perfect length for most resumes is one page. This is especially true if you are a new graduate or for anyone with less than 10 years job-related experience. As a general rule for more than 10 years professional, managerial or executive level experience and multiple achievements, a 1½ to 2 page resume is acceptable. Submitting a resume which is too long is damaging, considered by many to be discourteous, uninformed, arrogant and potentially unable to be concise in communication. The busy reader may simply be uninterested in the time investment demanded by the verbose material.

In addition, many Internet applications may restrict resume length by imposing character limitations. Where this happens, your resume may be literally "cut off" at the point of space limitation.

Too long?
Suggestions follow:

Task Statements
- Check for redundancies.
- Group similar tasks into single statements.
- Eliminate information that is too detailed or too elementary (allow for assumptions regarding inherent and routine tasks).
- Keep statements to one line.
- Shorten lines by choosing new words with less characters without losing impact.

Achievements
Achievements are extremely important and should not be eliminated. Analyze your statements. Make sure they are impressive and concisely stated. One to two sentences is ideal.

Education
If you are degreed you need not offer additional information regarding high school, seminars and/or workshops. You may elect to do so if these are job-related.

Optional Information
Review your format guidelines regarding optional information. Do not use this information unless it enhances your credentials.

Licenses and/or Certifications
Eliminate licenses and/or certifications that are not job-related.

Formatting
Work with margins, fonts, tabs and line wraps... but avoid overcrowding. A crowded resume presents an overwhelming appearance, discourages readers and promotes a negative response.

Too Short?
If your draft is significantly less than one page, you will need to add information. Review the optional categories, especially the Highlights of Qualifications section to make sure you have maximized this opportunity. Do your best to use these categories as they present an excellent opportunity for generating additional and very favorable information.

If your draft is only slightly short, and you are pleased with its content, you may simply try different spacing strategies to produce a full, one-page resume. Do not use larger than 12 pt font for standard text. Headings can use up to 14 pt standard fonts.

Visual Appeal

Whether electronic or print, these guidelines are essential:
♦ Keep the format simple. Do not complicate the appearance with too many fonts. Use bold lettering sparingly. Use bold, underlining and italics to help headings and key items of information stand out – create parallelism without confusion.
♦ Precede each task statement with a bullet point for clarity and easy reading.

Electronic Visual Appeal...
♦ Maintain versions in several software formats if possible. Review employer and job bank "apply on line" instructions for preferred formats and upload or email only that format. MS Word is still the most popular.
♦ Do not upload or copy/paste resumes which have complicated formatting or graphics coding. You'd be surprised how software can skew your resume and make it appear messy and unprofessional. Columns, lines, shading and templates can be skewed through technology. Only .pdf and similar locked graphics versions will protect the visualization of graphics.

Print Visual Appeal...
♦ Ensure wide margins and one to three blank lines between each section.
♦ Use standard letter size, high quality bond paper and matching envelopes. A color other than white is best. Most resumes are written on white paper, so yours will stand out if you use another color. An ivory/off-white, pale gray or buff will do the job nicely. Never use bright, pastel or dark colors. Recent surveys find ivory to be favored by most employers. (Artists and graphic artists are allowed and encouraged, however, to create a tasteful demonstration of their talent and skill through professional use of color, font and graphics.)
♦ Your name, address, phone number and email address should be on the same page as your resume. Never use a separate page for this information as this is awkward for filing and, more importantly, if the name page gets lost, your resume will be unidentifiable.
♦ Use two sheets of paper for two page resumes. Do not print on both sides of one piece of paper. Also, do not have your resume printed book-style. That is, a 17" x 11" sheet which gets folded down the middle so when opened, it makes up two attached, facing pages, each of 8 ½" by 11" size. These will generally get folded inside-out and are awkward for reading, filing and scanning into computer databases. Be certain that your name and page appear at the left top margin on consecutive pages.
♦ Proofread the resume before you send it out. Even a printing service can make a mistake. Check all words for correct spelling and punctuation for proper use. Errors show lack of attention to detail and carelessness.
♦ Do not enclose your resume in a plastic cover, report or file folder. These extras are cumbersome, too large for standard files, and impossible for scanners.

Submitting Your Resume

The manner in which you submit your resume depends entirely upon the prospective employer's preferences! At every step of the process, demonstrate respect for the company and attention to detail. If you are asked to email a resume, email it. If asked to submit through Internet technology, do so. Use personal delivery or postal mail only when specifically permitted or not instructed to use another means. While historically these means of resume submission were considered desirable, demonstrating extra effort and passion for the opportunity, today these invasive means are considered extra work for the employer and disrespectful to company process and efficiency. Resume processing and data warehousing is often electronic. Print copy often creates extra work for the employer... or ends up disqualified from candidacy.

If you have a contact to leverage, perhaps a team member, client or business associate of the prospective employer, the time to deploy this advantage is **after** you have submitted your resume through requested application protocol. (Of course, please be certain your contact is in good standing with the prospective employer before finding yourself "guilty by association.") With a credible contact to follow up for you, pointing to your resume submission as requested, and providing personal endorsement, you've enhanced your candidacy!

Following Up After Resume Submission

Today, resume follow up may actually disqualify you, so think twice before doing so!

Once your resume is submitted, continue to demonstrate respect for the company process and hiring authorities. Many employers will specifically state "No phone calls, please" or "Apply on line only." If you are not provided a name, title or email address to apply to, consider this a polite "don't call us, we'll call you" statement.

Employers today are often simply not staffed to receive large incoming communications via telephone or personal visit. It can be just as invasive as telemarketing, so be careful before infringing upon someone's time. Now, if the position you are applying for is telemarketing, following up without permission may actually demonstrate desirable job characteristics. Again, however, think twice even when applying for a sales role as many of today's business development opportunities are positioned upon relationship building as opposed to aggressive and invasive tactics. "Cold calls" can work for or against you. As soon as you have submitted your resume, you are auditioning for the role, so demonstrate only those characteristics which are the "keys to success" for the role to which you are applying.

If you have applied through technology and did not receive a success message, careful follow-up is permitted. In this case, use the contact info given and simply send a courteous and professional alert that you have applied but did not receive success message. Instead of requesting a response from the employer, expressly demonstrate concern for protocol and hiring authority time. Provide your contact information in the event your resume was not received in good order.

Follow-up is appropriate when you are provided a specific name, email address or title, and at no point have you been instructed to not follow up. Read every instruction carefully before making this assumption. Under these conditions, be certain to follow up. Make sure you contact when you say you will.

Bonus Section: The Cover Letter
STILL...The Best Kept Secret in the Job Search Process!

WHY A COVER LETTER?

Not every candidate uses the cover letter, and the very existence of a cover letter can immediately set you apart and keep you through "round 1" of candidate elimination. Some candidates use form or "Dear Employer" cover letters. This is sometimes worse than no cover letter at all and is expected to produce elimination no later than "round 2."

This document introduces your resume and you to the screening authority, whom most likely you have never met and who will make the decision about whether or not to continue granting you precious time. It is a screening team's responsibility to not waste company time by producing obviously disqualified candidates. What's interesting here is that if you are wrongfully disqualified, it likely goes undetected. Yet, if your candidacy is passed along and you're not an appropriate candidate, the error is noticed and the screening team is blamed. That is, it can be riskier to send you through than to disqualify you. Knowing this, use every competitive edge you can find.

The resume is a factual, impersonal and general record of your credentials and experience. Often, the resume wasn't even prepared by the candidate. The cover letter, however, can be a compelling individualized message targeting to a specific opportunity. The cover letter reinforces your interest.

In today's world of "shopping cart" job boards, employers cannot trust the serious intent and interest of any specific candidate. The cover letter answers to that concern and sets you apart... ahead of the competition!

The cover letter provides you opportunity to favorably influence the potential employer through strategic information and dynamic language, to motivate that person to grant you an interview... or at least phone screen. It affords you the opportunity to actually express passion and desirable behavioral characteristics essential to the position.

By learning the rules and applying certain specific strategies you will be able to write a dynamic and impressive cover letter. To assist you in this endeavor, we have provided the following information.

RULES OF ENGAGEMENT

Respect the Employer's Instruction

• If an employer is asking for electronic application through on-line templates, you MUST follow directions and use those templates precisely. Failing to do so will certainly set you apart -- but negatively, as someone who cannot or will not respect and follow instruction.

• If an employer provides an email address, your cover letter is your email message and your resume is the attachment.

• If an employer provides an on-line application method with any space/field for additional comments, copy and paste a targeted cover letter into that field.

Customize Your Cover Letter to Each Opportunity

• The cover letter must be tailored to fit each job for which you apply. This means that you must send an original cover letter each time you apply for a job. You will not need to re-write an entire new cover letter each time, but you will need to adjust the content so that it is specific to each job and/or employer.

• If you are enlisting the help of a professional service to write your resume, please don't let anyone else write your cover letter for you. "Form" cover letters are disqualified quickly. A professional resume writer who does not know this is probably not very effective.

Be Clear in Your Purpose and Exceed Expectations

The potential employer expects to learn three things from your cover letter.
1. To which position are you applying?
2. Why do you want the job? Why are you interested in the company? (To ensure you'll stick with it and dedicate to it.)
3. Do you meet the requirements better than your competition?

It is the ultimate goal of the resume/cover letter to get you the interview. Therefore, you must convince the reader that an interview with you is worth their time. Reading and sorting through a cluttered inbox of cover letters and resumes is a difficult task. Specific and relevant information will ease that task and greatly improve your chances for securing an interview.

FORMATTING STRATEGY & CONTENT

Length

Limit your letter to one page with plenty of "white space." Three to four brief paragraphs should be sufficient. Use a standard, professional business format. The same is true for an electronic version.

Visual Quality & Appeal

The quality should be just as professional as the resume. Spelling, grammar and punctuation must be correct. Use the same font style as the resume – or a font that is complimentary to and visually appealing alongside your resume. Fonts should be fairly standard print. "Arial," "Verdana" or a similar font would be very acceptable.

In print form, use matching stationery for cover letter, resume and envelopes. Use an off-white conservative color. According to employer survey, Ivory is preferred as professional with warmth. Light gray is 2nd most popular, especially a "warmer" shade of light gray. Unless you are applying to a graphics-related or aggressive sales-related opportunity, avoid bright colors.

Each section of the resume affords you a unique opportunity to personalize your message. In many cases you will be able to address your letter to a specific company and/or person. Your greatest opportunity to "grab" the reader's interest will be in your opening sentence. Start with a specific statement about the company or the person to which you are applying. Your middle paragraph(s) should present your personal qualifications as they relate to the position. Lastly, in your closing, you can personalize your interest in the position through summarizing statements of your credentials and also by asking for a meeting.

We'll start by discussing to whom you should be addressing your letter and follow with a detailed discussion of each section.

Addressee & Salutation

Wherever possible, address your letter to a specific person. There may be times when you do not know the name of the hiring company, much less the specific hiring authority. If you have a name and title, use them both with correct spelling. While Mr., Mrs., Ms., Dr. and other prefixes help, do not assume gender, as a mistake will hurt you.

If you are not responding to a recruitment but wish to apply to a specific employer, first visit the employer's website to search for instructions on how to apply or postings of available opportunities. Today, most employers prefer resumes submitted online. Please be respectful of this protocol.

Your salutation demonstrates your interaction style. If you do not have contact name or title to address, a safe salutation is "Dear Hiring Authority." The use of "Dear" is somewhat controversial but most often preferred by employers surveyed. Another choice will make a statement about you, so choose carefully. "Hiring Authority" demonstrates respect for your audience, and this is always a good start! It is not necessary to use a salutation if you have no contact information and it doesn't suit your style.

What's most important is to start out in salutation, attention line or first line of text identifying company name or job title. Should you fail to demonstrate this customization, your cover letter may be assumed a "form letter," and your letter and resume may lose the reader's interest.

Using Contacts, Professional Endorsements and References

If you know of someone held in high esteem by the hiring authority, by all means use that name in your cover letter. In doing so, please be certain this person has credibility with your resume/cover letter screener. Avoid the "guilty by association" syndrome. We strongly recommend that you respect the instructions of application/resume submission and do not use contacts in avoidance of this instruction. First apply through the recruiting company's preferred means, and then, if you have a credible contact willing, have that professional follow up to personally endorse you with the hiring authorities. Show respect for the process and respect for ALL people and instructions involved in the process!

First Paragraph

Establish a personal connection... prove and create interest. If possible, in your very first sentence, try to say something positive about the employer to which you are applying. This strategy not only flatters and creates positive bias with the reader, but also sets forth your sincere commitment to the company and begins to convince the reader of your potential to be a long term, enthusiastic and dedicated contributor to the organization. Today's employer invests substantially into the training of new hires. The average payback to the employer is approximately 7 months before they stop losing money from hiring you. Stability is a huge concern to employers.

Citing knowledge of the particular person or company will also demonstrate the extra effort and time you have devoted to learn about this particular company. This in itself should give you the advantage over other applicants. It will establish an immediate connection, as well as, illuminate your interest and sincerity regarding the position. If you have a referral or contact name in good standing to "drop," this is where you do so.

In that opening paragraph, it is critical that you identify the job title or field/department to which you are applying. This will 1) appropriately route your resume, 2) set forth your career focus (without which you are a less desirable candidate), and 3) attain the reader's favorable bias by making your message more clear and simple to understand. Starting your letter with personalized information about the company can be done fairly easily. Your best source for the most updated information is probably the Internet.

Middle Paragraph(s)

What can you bring to the job? One or two paragraphs should be used to discuss your credentials as they relate to the job requirements. Do not restate your resume, but use your brief explanation to mention job qualifications not detailed on your resume or briefly address that you fulfill each of the requirements presented. If possible, quickly restate those requirements without exceeding allowable cover letter length or being too redundant to your resume. The potential employer will be looking for a match between your qualifications and their job requirements. Your resume will reveal your credentials, so do not repeat your resume in detail but rather relevant summary statements. The reader wants that set forth as clearly and concisely as possible.

Whether you meet all the requirements or not, you must do your best to address each one. In doing so, please stick to statements which provide real information; that is, avoid statements such as "willing to be trained" or "quick learner." These have become meaningless clichés which detract from the credibility and newsworthiness of your cover letter. If possible, state specific job-related training or research which sets you apart from the competition. If you have nothing special to offer related to a job requirement, most employers agree it's better to avoid the mention. The prospective employer will be looking for very specific information and they will, most likely, be willing to do some training if most of these criteria can be met and you present "extraordinary" advantage in some other criteria. What might be "extraordinary" still needs to be job-related. These could be related skills, education, licensing/certification, recognition earned, selection to honorary responsibilities and/or quantifiable achievements.

If you have related experience that has been on a more personal basis such as hobbies, personal projects or volunteer work, then most likely, this information will not be on your resume. This is your chance to include that information.

Any time you can add "something extra" to your cover letter you will be adding additional value to your credentials which could also translate into additional value for the company. Another very positive outcome could be your portrayal of yourself through favorable behavioral traits including but not limited to work ethic, ambition, dedication, reliability, flexibility, collaboration, commitment and/or perseverance.

Last Paragraph: The Closing

This is where you summarize your qualifications, thank the employer, and respectfully ask for the interview. If you are not applying on-line but rather to a specific person, mention your follow up here… and then be certain to follow up exactly as you promised.

Follow-up Is Appropriate When… You are provided a specific name, email address or title, and at no point have you been instructed to not follow up. Read every instruction carefully before making this assumption. Under these conditions, be certain to follow up. Make sure you contact when you say you will. Below are examples of cover letter statements:

"I will contact you next week to ascertain your preferred method of moving forward."

"I will be in Chicago from August 15th through the 18th. I will contact your office next week to see if it would be convenient for you to meet with me during that time."

Follow-up Is Not Appropriate When... You are not provided a specific name, email address or title, but rather an on-line database form or Internet application for which to apply, and you have received instruction somewhere which deters follow up. Examples include "No phone calls, please," or "We ask you to apply by Internet only." The only candidates who should consider contact beyond these requests are those required to aggressively ignore communication protocol on the job, e.g. salespeople not responsible for relationship building. Respecting the time and instruction of others you are applying to report to is critical to presenting yourself positively and remaining in candidacy. Demonstrating attention to detail is always important!

Submitting your resume for consideration is an entire process, and each stage of that process has its direct effect upon your candidacy. Your attention to and compliance with employer instruction, expressed or implied, both make statements about you. Be certain you are making statements which reinforce your appropriateness to the position for which you are applying. As in every communication, it is not just what you say... but how you say it!

Please find additional reference materials at AskHRS.com.

www.ingramcontent.com/pod-product-compliance
Lightning Source LLC
Chambersburg PA
CBHW081239170526
45165CB00009B/3111

* 9 7 8 1 4 3 9 2 3 0 1 6 9 *